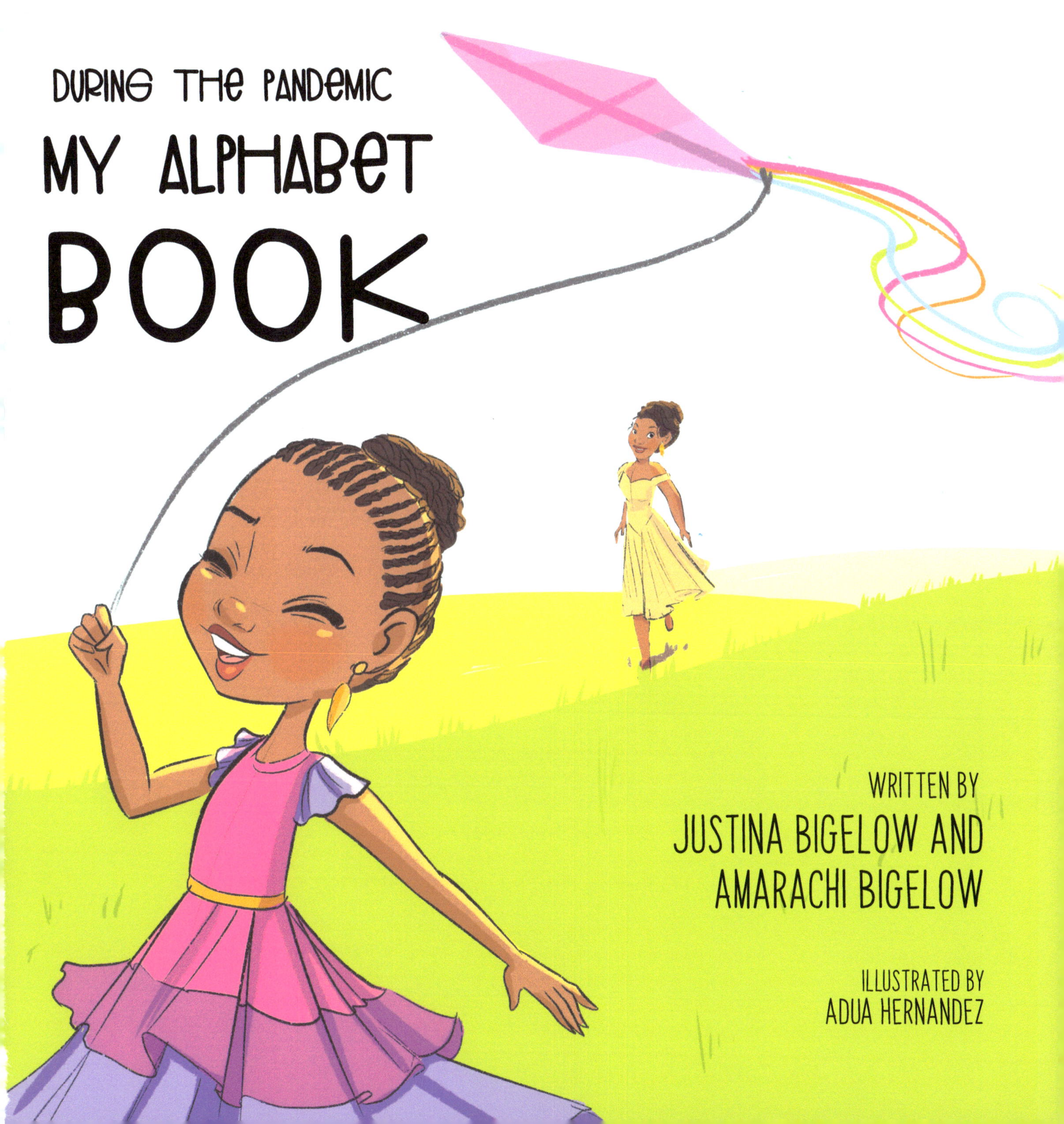

DURING THE PANDEMIC

MY ALPHABET BOOK

WRITTEN BY
JUSTINA BIGELOW AND
AMARACHI BIGELOW

ILLUSTRATED BY
ADUA HERNANDEZ

During the Pandemic: My Alphabet Book

For information address
Small House Publishing
22 Baily Road
Yeadon, PA 19050

www.welcometosmallhouse.com
www.justinabigelow.com

ISBN: 978-1-7348427-7-7

Library of Congress Control Number: 2021923793

First Edition

INTRODUCTION

In 2020, the whole world was hit by the COVID-19 pandemic. COVID-19 is caused by a coronavirus called SARS-CoV-2, which usually causes an upper respiratory tract illness that may lead to death. It is contagious, so we were forced to quarantine for safety. Since my daughter and I were home with no-where to go for over a year, we decided to write this alphabet book to share with you what we did during the pandemic of 2020 - 2021.

DEDICATION

I dedicate this book to my daughter, Amarachi Pearl Bigelow. She is very close to my heart; my whole world changed the day she was born. I also want to dedicate this book to my husband, Herbert Bigelow. He is a great husband and father – he is my ROCK! That is, he is and has been very supportive in all my life endeavors. Finally, to my brother, Godwin Onuoha, a certified nurse practitioner, who went to work daily supporting people who were suffering with the virus, putting his own life at risk. He has been a father-figure to me since we lost our parents.

Aa

We made our own apple cider drink.

Bb

We wrote a book together.

Cc

We learned a lot about COVID-19.

Dd

We danced to our favorite music under the disco ball.

Ee

We did lots of exercise.

Ff

We wore face masks
everywhere we went.

Gg

We grew flowers in our garden.

Hh

We stayed home the whole day!

Ii

We ate lots of ice cream.

Jj

We played online jeopardy with family and friends.

Kk

We made and flew kites.

Ll

We studied and learned different languages.

Mm

We used a ukulele to make music.

Nn

We took lots of naps and got lots of rest.

We made tropical orange punch.

Oo

Pp

We painted many pictures.

Qq

We stayed home and
quarantined for safety reasons.

Rr

We made rainbow slime!

Ss

We used hand sanitizer a lot!

Tt

We gathered lots of toilet paper to use during quarantine.

Uu

We used the internet to stay united with our families around the world.

Vv

We took the COVID-19 vaccine.

We went for a walk almost every day.

Ww

Xx

We enjoyed playing video games on our Xbox.

Yy

We did lots of yoga.

Zz

We used Zoom as a platform for learning and communication.

What did you do during the pandemic?
Draw a picture.

GLOSSARY

Cc

COVID-19- a short name for the coronavirus disease announced in 2019.

Nn

Naps- a short sleep during the day.

Qq

Quarantine- being kept away from others to avoid the spread of disease.

Ss

Sanitizer- a product used for killing germs.

Vv

Vaccine- a substance given to people by injection to prevent them from getting sick from a particular disease.

Xx

Xbox- a type of video game console.

Zz

Zoom- a video conference meeting site.

ABOUT THIS BOOK

During the Pandemic: My Alphabet Book, is designed to teach children to recognize letters and sounds of the alphabet while sharing our experience during the 2020 pandemic.

MEET THE AUTHORS

Hello! My name is Justina Bigelow, I grew up in Nigeria, on the continent of Africa. I currently live in Philadelphia, PA. I hold a master's degree of Education in Early Childhood and Special Education from Lincoln University. I am a Pennsylvania certified teacher, and I am currently pursuing a doctoral degree in Early Childhood Leadership and Advocacy with Walden University. After 5+ years in the education field, I realized that I have a passion for improving reading skills with my students.

During the COVID-19 pandemic, my daughter, Amarachi, and I authored a book entitled, During the Pandemic: My Alphabet Book. It is a simple alphabet book written to help young readers develop their understanding of the alphabetic principle and explore alphabet letters and sounds.

If you have any questions, do not hesitate to contact me at

justinabigelow@gmail.com

Hello! My name is Amarachi Pearl Bigelow. I was born and raised in Philadelphia. I am currently in middle school. I enjoy drawing, painting, and playing ukulele. I live in Philadelphia. Writing a book together with my mother, Justina Bigelow, was a fun thing to do. And I believe every early reader will enjoy the vibrant and creative illustrations. I hope to author many more books someday.

www.ingramcontent.com/pod-product-compliance
Ingram Content Group UK Ltd.
Pitfield, Milton Keynes, MK11 3LW, UK
UKHW061030310726
14089UKWH00009B/180
9781734842777